Maverick Mindset Skills

GET YOUR MIND SET

Jay Arnott

GET YOUR MIND SET: Maverick Mindset Skills © 2020 Jay Arnott

All Rights Reserved.

No part of this book shall be reproduced, copied, or transmitted electronically, by any means including recording, storage systems, or photocopying, without first securing written permission by the author.

This book is presented as an insight into the Maverick Mindset and offers suggestions for mindset change and self-help. All readers are responsible for their actions within the jurisdiction and laws of the countries in which they abide.

Whilst all attempts have been made to provide accurate information and character anonymity, neither the author nor publisher assumes responsibility for similarities to actual people, errors, omissions, or inappropriate misuse of the book's content.

For more information, please visit www.jayarnott.com.

Interpretation of maverick taken from www.Dictionary.com (date accessed: 24.06.20)

Cowboy cover image by Neonbrand Marketing at Unsplash.com.

Blue brick background by Wesley Tingey at Unsplash.com.

ISBN: 9798653158209

MAVERICK [MAV-ER-IK, MAV-RIK]

Noun

1. *Southwestern U.S.* an unbranded calf, cow, or steer, especially an unbranded calf that is separated from its mother.

2. a lone dissenter, as an intellectual, an artist, or a politician, who takes an independent stand apart from his or her associates:

3. a person pursuing rebellious, even potentially disruptive, policies or ideas:

Adjective

Unorthodox, unconventional, nonconformist.

DO something different.

CONTENTS

Introduction	1
The Maverick Mindset Qualities	17
Intention	18
Positivity	20
Curiosity	21
Persistence	22
Don't Give a Shit	23
Create Success Before It Happens	25
Framing	25
Frontloading	27
When You Come and See Me	32
Priming	34
Imaginary Lemons	38
Monitor Growth	40
Square Mindset vs. The Maverick Mindset	43
Square Thinking	43
Maverick Mindset	47
Switch Your Emotions	49
Maverick Mindset Switch	50

Reframing	55
Switching Neuro Levels to a Maverick Mindset	59
Information Sorting	62
Logical Levels	63
An Exercise in Using Logical Levels	66
Logical Types	69
Uncertainty, Your Friend	74
Don't Fear the Reaper	75
Mourning Celebrations	78
Necessity Is Essential	80
Future Diary	86
Maverick Mindset Quiz	88

INTRODUCTION

Hey, Jay here. Welcome to this book, which is the first in a series of books about the Maverick Mindset Skills principles. All these skills can be explicitly learnt, and the goal of each book is to introduce you to the practical skills and the thinking that surrounds them.

My hope is to present each book of these principles in a tasty but inherently more salubrious manner than a box of carefully selected Belgian chocolates whereby each concept retains its own taste and texture as part of the greater box. In these preliminary pages, I want to talk about mindset. It's a word that gets thrown around all the time.

Mindset.

Is it setting, resetting, changing the algorithm, or the software of your mind?

What is it?

Recently, the popularity of the word mindset undoubtedly came from the work of Professor Carol Dweck. She's done Ted Talks and written a book called Mindset. It's pretty good, I read it whilst on holiday in the Algarve in Portugal two years back, and it got me thinking. Much of what Dweck outlines in her book resonated with me. She talks about the difference between a fixed and a growth mindset. After reading it, I began to formulate my own interpretations. Suddenly I could relate her insights in that book with certain clients I had worked with. In particular, clients like those who had experienced one failure and then chosen to adopt a fixed mindset and stay stuck within the context of, 'I fail therefore I am.' Clients that saw failure as the end game rather than feedback. Dweck also inferred that a fixed mindset can undermine those who achieve success too. People with a specific talent often chose to rest on their laurels rather than see it as an opportunity for further growth. For them, the buck stopped there. A person with a fixed mindset was more likely to spend their time documenting their talents than developing them. In contrast, those with a growth mindset believed their basic abilities could be developed through dedication and hard work. It is the growth mindset that interests me most, because curiosity, creativity, and questioning boundaries are key qualities of the maverick mind.

When I first heard the expression Growth Mindset I thought, here we go again—another American fad where all the geniuses that have excelled at their sport, art, business, or academia are American. Here we go—another American buzzword where growth is about how much material abundance you can acquire. This type of outlook had never been my focus. In my life, I had always preferred less material, a degree of minimalistic simplicity, and as a maverick I preferred scarcity to accumulating lots of objects that weigh me down. I preferred to be agile exploring new and exciting environments and have the freedom to move unfettered at will.

So I assumed that the growth mindset was about creating more massive financial impact and acquiring possessions, but I was wrong. The growth mindset was in fact right up my street and is about getting the electricity in our brain firing off and wiring off in new directions to expand our neural connections. The aim of which is to metamorphose these into new skills and behaviours.

One common thread throughout Mindset which hit a sweet spot with me and echoed my experience with coaching clients is the idea that failure is a continual learning path. People who do reach the very top of their game embrace it as such. Although these types of people may have several debilitating setbacks on their journey, they kept going, believing in one thing: How can I do better? Just remember this the next time you fail or something goes wrong: what can you do better? How can you do things differently next time to get a different result? How will you deploy more creative solutions to keep moving forward?

Right up until the end of your life, you'll always be learning and growing. The moment you stop and decide to stay fixed your momentum grinds to a halt. You lose your bounce, become static and, yes, you'll probably feel like a failure as you feel yourself sliding in the opposite direction. As you slide, instead of growth, you feel your world beginning to contract.

On this journey of growth, sometimes you need a clear plan, sometimes you don't. I don't believe in the law of attraction either. Drawing from my own personal experience, the law of attraction is an imbalanced view of the romantic perspective, a warm and dreamy whole-world view that does not account for the cold scientific part-whole realities. When adopting the Maverick Mindset, 'the law of the attraction is physical action,' and if your intention is strong, you are willing to put in effort and flex along the way you'll acquire new skills and grow.

'It's my life, it never ends,' sang Mark Hollis, lead singer of Talk Talk. Much the same can be said about the task of managing our mindset. It never ends. In fact, the word mindset itself creates an illusion that our mind can be permanently set when the opposite is true. Our minds remain open at all hours to new suggestions, and in every context, we can always learn more. Some humans don't have the desire to do so but luckily most people do and within the past decade, due to books like Mindset, the concept of a growth mindset has become super trendy, but growth is an ancient ideal that encompasses our emotional and spiritual potential, and to embrace growth we must learn how to tack upwind and move our emotions out from the doldrums whilst keeping a gentle hand on the tiller. If we do this, we will soon be adept at changing our emotional and mental state to transform our behaviour.

Making such changes are entirely possible and we can do this at will using various mindset skills which include but are not limited to: self-hypnosis, Neuro-linguistic programming (NLP), meditation and mindfulness, psychosensory techniques, bilateral brain games and physiology exercises, even dancing and sport. Of course, there are also faith-based methodologies that rely heavily on story, metaphor, and myth to amplify our sensory perceptions into a belief system, but we'll leave that out of the deal for now. The thing is, you don't need all these approaches, and you'd be ill-equipped with just one. What you need is not one quick fix that some well-marketed guru has a vested interest in and states is the panacea for all of life's ills. No, you need a variety of techniques because people and environments are dynamic, they change all the time, and some of these patterns will work better than others within specific contexts. Some have a more general scope, and most are a development of something else. You might not need any techniques at all, but in my experience, mindset-altering processes could save our health services millions in terms of time, energy, and money by preventing all manner of symptoms. Sometimes, all you need is a swift positive suggestion, an internal dialogue shift, in some cases downright bloody-mindedness or the awareness to know when to listen to yourself and when not, when to listen to others and when to tell them to shut the fuck up; when to listen to your environment and the awareness to know when to fight, flee, or move on.

Having a creative mind helps. If you haven't got one, find one, for knowing you'll find a way even if you can't see one is the Maverick Mindset in action. Cultivating a Maverick Mindset allows you to do what works best. Suggestion, too, plays a major part in our lives, and we are surrounded by it in all of its subliminal forms, from what our parents say to what our politicians and advertisers insert. If you think the use of suggestion to get a result is unethical, let me tell you: everything is a suggestion, from the colours you wear to the environment you inhabit. Music on TV programmes is a fine example of suggestion at work. You may remember the soundtrack from movies like Stephen Spielberg's Jaws or the clown music that comes on TV. As soon as an innocent protagonist steps onto the screen and we hear lolloping trombone octaves this instantly suggests that the person in the frame is an oaf, even if they haven't done anything silly. Remove the music, remove the suggestion, and if you remove the music from Jaws, forget it.

Introduction

Suggestion is everywhere, incremental, obvious, on the billboards of a political party's campaign bus plastered with pictures of queueing immigrants and the phrase, 'we're being flooded.' It's there when you're browsing YouTube and come across a Tommy Robinson video where he speaks confidently with great passion, tonality, and charisma about the same topic and spouts lots of apparent facts. Later that day, you find yourself in a pub where you have a sad conversation about a friend of yours losing his job. Meanwhile, in the corner, you overhear a group of young men having a heated conversation about the rising population of immigrants in your town. On your way home, a group of women in Burkas ignore you as you cross the road and boom the suggestions are compounded.

This is how dogmas form, through the layering and stacking of suggestion, which comes mostly from our peers, parents, and places (environment). Suggestion feeds into our five senses, but how aware are you of your own susceptibility to the suggestions in your environment? What process do you use to filter them in and out? What suggestions have you allowed to become part of your unconscious conditioning? How do you consciously project your own positive suggestions out into your environment?

If you haven't begun the adventure that is changing your mindset already, and you feel a victim of the suggestions around you, then stop to think about what alternative sensory suggestions you could be giving to yourself instead, because once your awareness increases, the dial shifts, and you become a maestro at directing your mind. As you begin harnessing the nature of your uniquely authentic mind, you embrace the true maverick spirit. You burn previous learnings and maps in an instant and abandon old theologies in a heartbeat in order to get a result. As a maverick, you know when to listen and when not. As a maverick, you don't follow the rules or the crowd. You do what works. Do what it takes. By any means possible.

One thing I have discovered through coaching hundreds of clients obsessed with achieving a goal is that the thing they originally wanted to achieve (the initial perceived pain) was never the thing that was actually holding them back. In other words, ninety percent of the time the perceived goal at the front of a client's conscious mind was never the actual goal of their deeper unconscious need.

For example, some clients believed that in order to attain deep satisfaction all they needed was more money, a new car, a different partner, or some weird quick fix to release them from misery. Yet in almost every case, there was always some kind of mental block, a psychological or emotional barrier holding them back; an impasse which came with a whole range of assumptions, beliefs, and destructive thought patterns which some may call by that other hip label: Imposter Syndrome. Even though these people had initially sought help, some chose to keep a fixed mindset. Some had past traumas that needed clearing. Others had erroneous undoubtedly dangerous beliefs about the world, but beneath the surface noise and groans of discomfort low-esteem and self-sabotage were rife. Perhaps the most common theme among aspirant business professionals was, 'I just need more cash,' thinking that more money would solve everything, but the opposite was often true. First, they had to get out of their own way.

That's why removing mindset blocks is so important—because if we don't remove them, they stay with us until the end of our days. In truth, we think we have a grip on this thing called reality, but our version of it is nothing more than a well-filtered construct based on historic maps and the conditioning of our upbringing. What each of us considers reality is only a lens through which we choose to view the world, a lens that varies from person to person. World beliefs have the potential to be malleable or set depending on what we choose. The maverick views beliefs as malleable, because that's what they are in the plasticity of our brain.

Behold! A shift is occurring.

People are getting increasingly disheartened with expensive visits to psychologists, years of feeble counselling, and outdated psychotherapy techniques that take thousands of years just to tell them what they already know. People have become bored of talking about their mindset blocks and their problems in a way that doesn't make their issues disappear. People are expressing disappointment at pharma-funded, clock-watching doctors who administer drugs as their first point of call. People are getting pissed off with pharmaceutical monopolies and their dependency-inducing medications that block the body's natural ability to heal and don't alleviate their symptoms. They don't want Victorian methods, but they don't want corporate America either.

People are crying out for a new approach that, methodologically, is actually quite old. A maverick understands that for environmental change to occur and to move from the norm, rocking the boat is an essential prerequisite. Many fellow coaches and alternative practitioners have fostered what I call a punk rock spirit to initiate such change. Instead of idling on their arses, they rejected what they had been hypnotised on and spoon-fed by society for so long. In true D.I.Y spirit, they decided to go it alone, choosing ownership and action over apathy.

The truth is that nothing holds you back—except you. For some people, a mindset shift can be gradual and take months, weeks, days, or even years; others can rid themselves of a lifetime of gridlock in hours or minutes simply by applying Maverick Mindset Skills. You can do this, too.

This is a highly practical book and works on the principle of dance first, think later. We encourage you to nurture this know-nothing state; that is, to keep a beginner's mind which will allow you to reflect more critically later.

By way of caution, this book is not another 'research has shown that a small group of students at Harvard and Yale expressed certain behaviours under a controlled double-blind experiment that was made into a highly respected white paper.' There will be scant citations from 'experts,' both because I want to call out the guru in you, and also because a maverick knows that real wisdom comes from direct experience, not from somebody else's analytical critique or case study. Not that there's anything wrong with analytical case studies; it just ain't maverick that's all.

Nor will this book be vandalised by cliché and I have exercised conscientious restraint not to produce another cliché-ridden set of works smattered with Freudulent citations and the obligatory quotes of Lao Tzu.

After all, this book is supposed to be maverick.

The Maverick Mindset is supposed to be about doing things differently to get different results. It's about questioning the norm and choosing a positive state of Cartesian doubt. Beneath the core thinking the Maverick Mindset imparts practical skills we can immediately put into action, overseen by Seven Core Principles.

Get Your Mind Set

This first section is about how to frame success in advance with others, enhance your success, and develop a working Maverick Mindset to help you get in the frame and stay in the game.

Disruption

This is about neurologically disrupting the mindsets that hold us back. Through activities, exercises and games we disrupt, dissolve, and dissipate states like fear, anxiety, and self-sabotage.

Unconscious Results

We can develop an alliance with our unconscious mind to place trust in the unconscious processes, achieve unconscious competence, and get faster, more accurate results.

Metaphor

We can work with our presenting somatic metaphors, symbolism, visual dreamscapes, and totems to transform our perceptions and create powerful changes in the reality of our daily lives.

Future Focus

This is where we release past associations with failure and replace them with a compelling future alternatives and reverse-engineer.

The BIG Pause

Stop the hamster wheel and get off. Stop the world, learn how to lose anxiety and the worry response by creating a BIG Pause and find your peace in the gap between stimulus and response.

Humour

Humour dissolves fixed states and carries us toward convalescence; it keeps our internal organs pink, gives life meaning and a positive rosy outlook. Humour is serious shit.

Maverick Mindset Skills has my angles and insights on how to access the Maverick Mindset quickly through a philosophy and a variety of Maverick Mindset skills that you can develop and apply yourself. These are effective techniques for wellbeing and mental health that can be used in contexts of coaching and therapeutic change which anyone can use. Even an old lady sitting on the bus could use them, but she may not know about them yet, as they are not so widely distributed in the public domain on health services or mainstream news. Some of the techniques belong to others, to whom I give credit and thanks, some of the processes are my own.

Marco Polo once gasped on his deathbed words to the effect of, 'never stop learning,' meaning for organic growth to occur we must never stop moving forward. The choice is yours to step outside your comfort zone and challenge unwanted blocks and beliefs. Keep your mind on the prize but, as you read, please bear in mind that the principles are always far more than techniques. Work out how a process might be working for you. How you can blend that with other processes so that you remain flexible. Set your intention. Focus on something specific that is holding you back which you can either remove or improve during the course of this potentially life-changing interaction. See Maverick Mindset Skills as a kind of mind yoga supported by alternative thinking that's also about employing a Karate Kid, wax on, wax off, mentality. If you don't physically apply a skill, you'll never have anything to base your judgement on and sometimes what you are practising may seem silly. Fear not. Like Daniel in that movie, with a little practice, many of these skills will morph into unconscious behaviours when you are least expecting it. Much like the Buddhist philosophy a Maverick Mindset can be seen as:

1. A path towards fearlessness and positive emotion.
2. A radical way of changing the world by starting with ourselves.
3. Founded on direct experience, not blind belief.

One key variant however is the complete rejection of convention where needed. Not blind angst or rebellion but the awareness-driven ability to question everything presented to us. If something works, great; if it doesn't, we challenge it, question it, or try something else.

Every single person I have ever met who has reached the pinnacle of their success, whether this was financial freedom, having a happy family, winning in sport or business, or something else has exercised especially diligent attention on developing new skills. Although they may not have initially intended to do so, they took absolute responsibility for managing their own mind. Of course they had a game plan, a strategy, or business plan, but the first thing they needed was mindset. The square mindset, which you'll learn about later, does exactly what it says on the tin, it keeps you boxed in at the point of no change but the maverick mind on the other hand curiously requests, 'What can I do differently to get different results?'

As a last enticement before you dive into the book, let me describe where you are headed and what you can expect when you begin to apply these principles and techniques. As a maverick, you don't rely on external forces to tell you what you can and can't do, what you should or shouldn't do, how you should behave, or what in the outside world should make you happy because you live life on your terms and you trust each process you involve yourself in.

Don't believe the hype.

Remain eternally aware of the hypnosis society places on you, and reject most of it. Connect with your authentic self by creating your own positive autosuggestions and mindset strategies to rearrange your mental furniture and remove any blocks or baggage.

Have no desire in being 'the best version of yourself,' like the script that others are following, just be who you are and always have been before you picked up any shit along the way.

Embrace the meme that you are the author of your own story and you are enjoying writing it, for you are the guru, the authority, and whilst you learn from others and give back, you show up, own up, and stay benevolently solid at the centre of your world. Grab life by the balls, learn new skills, and sharpen your mind until it gleans like a diamond. Regrets, you'll have a few, but more than this you'll have the gumption to say, 'I did it my way.'

Got a BIG idea that you are struggling to get confident, focused, and clear on?

Check out my walkthrough training, 'Certainty: a Crash Course in Confidence' on the Maverick Mindset Skills Resources page:

http://bit.ly/MaverickMindsetSkillsFreeResources

THE MAVERICK MINDSET QUALITIES

See first with your mind, then with your eyes, and finally with your body.

- Yagyu Munenori

Get your Mind Set introduces the Maverick Mindset and is about moving your mind into different frames for success. Inside this book, you will learn about the Maverick Mindset, what it is, how to apply it, the benefits of applying it, and how to quickly switch from unhelpful states to positive emotional states and creative contrarian thinking. I also give you practical tools to help you monitor your mind to deal with ambiguity and sort complex information more easily. I'll show you how to set specific mindset frames that build expectation for better results. I coach you on the qualities needed to sustain the Maverick Mindset and how to create success in the mind before a physical event occurs. Essentially, this book is about doing things differently. So, look forward to this as a little pep talk from me about how to get creative and how to get your mind laser-focused, razor sharp, and crystal clear, but before we dive in wholeheartedly here's the glue that binds all this gold sparkled shit together, a set of wee precepts to help you stay in the frame and stay in the game. A cluster of convenient beliefs that will help you think differently and improve your results. For brevity's sake, I've narrowed it down to five Maverick Mindset qualities. Number one is:

Intention

Milton Erickson, the acclaimed psychiatrist and medical hypnotist, once said, 'A goal without a date is just a dream,' so specificity helps, and a true maverick knows their intention.

One of my intentions is writing. Some days, even though I am riddled with doubt and exhaustion from what feels like hard manual labour due to my glacially slow typing skills and terrible grammar, as soon as I check in with my end intention (the finished book), the pain slips away and I feel more aligned with the process.

Similarly, whenever anybody asks me about the subject of canoeing, I know my eyes light up and you can't stop me from talking, envisioning rivers, and moving my arms demonstratively as if I am there because I feel rock-solid, certain inside, with zero doubt.

Another strong intention of mine is to move to Portugal. It's a place I long to be because recently I went there on holiday, I love it, and I made a commitment to spend more time there.

So, when I say the word PORTUGAL you can see my physiology change. My inner Latino appears. I have no Latin blood whatsoever, but when I talk about Portugal my body opens up, and I start gesticulating with gusto as I see the colours and feel the thrill inside me of Portugal. Throughout the distractions of daily life, the feeling of Portugal drives me on.

Which brings me to you.

What's your intention?

What's drives you forward?

What comes to mind that has a strong somatic association for you?

Is it your children?

A holiday?

A different environment?

Why you are on this journey?

What do you deeply desire?

It is important to know your intention and attach meaning and compelling emotion to it in the form of thoughts, images, and feelings, to make it strong. Keep it really clear and simple. That way, your unconscious mind will more readily accept it.

See intention as your guiding light.

The first Maverick mindset quality is Intention. That's it. Know your intention.

Positivity

Quality number two is Positivity. Being a Maverick means you can bounce back quickly and stay in the positive frame. If something negative happens, you quickly flip it with a click of the fingers, a kick of the leg, or an Ubershake to prohibit unhelpful feelings. Ubershakes are physical shake-offs. They are a way to reset an unproductive emotional state by literally shaking everything off, but you mustn't do them by halves. That's why they're called Ubershakes and not simply Shakes. When humans get hurt, thoughts get trapped in our bodies and our energy gets needlessly consumed, but as Mavericks, we interrupt the process so that we can introduce positivity into the space.

That's the second Maverick Mindset quality, Positivity.

Curiosity

Quality number three is a topic that most mavericks that I've spoken to have all mentioned without fail. These are successful people who have lived by their own rules and created great satisfaction—people I've spoken to in person and people I've interviewed on my podcast—personal developers with an incessant desire for growth.

Mavericks like these all have what I would call an explorer spirit, a creative streak which allowed them to remain curious, and a phrase that kept surfacing time and again during our interviews was, 'Let's see.' Taking the 'see what happens' approach helped them to keep their desire fresh and allowed them to reflect quickly on failings to bring them forward as lessons for growth. These individuals did not allow themselves to be conditioned by other people's writings or discoveries, their ideas linked directly to their own experience. Neither did they view 'try' as the weak word so many perceived as inclusive of failure. Curiously and creatively, they tried out new things and opened the door to discovery, feedback, and new possibilities.

'Ok, let's give this a try,' they'd announce with a smirk as if this and the other phrase, 'See what happens' was part of their unconscious internal dialogue. They did not sit back, procrastinate, or create destructive, self-fulfilling prophecies or anxious assumptions about future events. No, they used a childlike curiosity as a constant feedback loop for improvement. As mavericks, we must unlearn the educational conditioning handed to us by society so we can return to this state of not knowing. We don't need information first. First we need direct experience. Then, through reflection, we can later catalogue and code those experiences if necessary.

Just there, I touched on the know nothing state. Some people call this working from a blank slate or the beginner's mind. It's perfectly normal to wake up in the morning with a deep desire that you want something but to not know what it is. It is incredibly common to know what you want but have no idea how to go about getting it. You may lack skills or confidence, maybe you're unable to strike a vision or associate strong feelings to a deep sense of need. It doesn't matter. All you need is curiosity and the belief that through creative flexibility somehow you'll get there. All that matters is that you have a germ of an idea, a strong intention, and a mind that remains open to the beyond. Remember to ask, 'What if?' in the positive frame. Adopt 'See what happens,' playfully, give things a try, take the first step. Go, be curious, see what happens.

Curiosity – the third Maverick Mindset quality

Persistence

Quality number four is Persistence.

Persistence is about not giving up. Never giving up. No. Not ever. Never.

Not necessarily in a YEAH BABY! gleaming-toothed, territorial, male-chest-beating silverback gorilla, bodybuilder on steroids, Tony Robbins kind of way. No, this is more about possessing a serene belief and positive, patient, persistence. Resilience is central to this quality; having the ability to fall down, bounce back like a rubber ball, and keep going.

Even when things go wrong, a maverick keeps going because when our intention is clear, we embrace positivity, curiosity, and are willing to 'see what happens' along the path of our highest intention, nothing can stand in our way.

The fourth Maverick mindset quality is persistence, the ability to readjust and continue.

Don't Give a Shit

Quality number five is perhaps the most important quality of all.

The one thing that holds people back from making a change or creating the life of their dreams.

Judgement.

Judgement comes in the form of negative self-criticism and prejudging the criticism from others. And it goes by different names, some call it fear, self-sabotage, Imposter Syndrome. Whatever you call it, stop. Stop right now. A Maverick Mindset means you care so much about making a positive difference that you really don't give a shit (what others think of you). You care so much about fulfilling your purpose and making an impact that you really, really don't give a shit.

Number five is Don't Give a Shit.

Down the road, in the Disruption and Unconscious Results books, which form part of the seven modules in the Mindset Skills Academy online coaching programme, I offer simple induction scripts and audios to help cut off your critical mind and get you into a receptive state ready to accept profound positive suggestion. I even have one called Do Not Give a Shit.

> Get your Do Not Give a Shit positive autosuggestion audio here on the Maverick Mindset Skills Resources page:
>
> http://bit.ly/MaverickMindsetSkillsFreeResources

So those are five key qualities of the Maverick Mindset.

Intention, Positivity, Curiosity, Persistence and Don't Give a Shit.

CREATE SUCCESS BEFORE IT HAPPENS

Setting positive high expectations in your own or your client's mind is paramount and without doubt is a highly regarded skill of the Maverick Mindset. If you're a coach or business professional, this could mean setting expectations and establishing boundaries when you first begin to work with a client. It could be an intake form, a two-minute video, a story, your branding, the clothes you wear, a foreword or introduction to a book, or a ten-minute triage assessment with a client before a longer strategy call to assess the parameters of your service and set your rules of engagement.

Framing

If communication is the response that you get, the purpose of setting a frame in communication is to change the meaning to enhance our success.

All meaning is context dependent, whether the behaviour is perceived as valuable or as bad depends on the context or frame in which we have chosen to view it. See framing as a lens through which you consciously choose to view the world. Framing is exactly what it says on the tin. A frame is a deliberately closed perspective in which to create a desired experience. That's why we sometimes refer to it as a closed frame.

For example, we could set up a closed possibility frame where we adopt an 'As if' attitude, as if a miracle has occurred and suddenly all things are possible. This could be a provocative frame through which we challenge and question our current beliefs. The frame could be a humorous or a solution-focused frame. Using closed frames like these help define the rules of engagement, establish boundaries and restrictions that help us focus, thus laying the groundwork for a potential reframes of experience.

Framing, as you will come to know, as in the frames above, are generally closed frames.

Frames can be open too.

Open frames, are where the rules of engagement are open. An open frame is literally a non-specified blank sheet with no closed frame that is the equivalent to a curiosity frame of 'Let's see.'

Open frames are frames of spontaneous discovery.

Frontloading

Frontloading is a tool we can store in our arsenal to improve our performance through expectation-building. If you are an NLPer you may look upon frontloading as a type of future pace. If the law of attraction is your thing, you could see frontloading as the precursor to manifesting your vision. Frontloading can be used as a form of mental dress rehearsal to prepare you for a future event. See it as a pre-frame where you assume the mindset, skills, and behaviours of future contexts. The great thing about it is that you can fast-forward, pause, and play it in real time, as if the event has already happened, to kick-start unconscious competence in the brain, it is something I used all the time for canoe sports coaching and personal development outdoors.

Nowadays in the UK, there seems to be less emphasis on young people venturing into the outdoors to discover their inner self. If there is any value placed on outdoor activities in schools, it seems centred around wham-bam cheap thrills or sport competition. Back in the day, and I am talking late 80s-90s, with the various outdoor personal development charities I worked for, there was an inclination towards development training. This wasn't merely taking kids into the outdoors so they could let off steam. No, it was a more carefully calibrated approach where young people could grow from the inside out, outside-in. Transferable learning was huge at the time, how skills and mindset challenges learnt in the outdoors could transfer into everyday urban lives. This inner growth was at the forefront of our minds and was supported beautifully by the outdoor environment, and a few of us held the view: how can we preserve earth if young people have no direct access to nature? Back then, we embraced David Kolb's learning cycle of Plan, Do, Review, reapplying what we'd learnt along the way. We put this model on steroids and made it a part of our ethos. Active Reviewing was big, and proponents like Roger Greenaway who extoled it were celebrated. On my bookshelf, I still have a little red book by John Hunt and Penny Hitchin, Creative Reviewing, which I would never sell for the world because it is such a gem of cartoons and activities spelled out simply in about seventy-five pages. Active reviewing is the reflection process that takes place after a physical group problem-solving activity. Be as creative as you like, use re-enactment as a group, play a game, construct a visualisation, a story or a poem, even a piece of art to help solidify learning.

At this time, outdoor leaders I worked with shared a belief that reviewing should be valued as important as the actual physical group activity but the reality materialising was that, due to a developing fervent interest, we were beginning to value it more so, and the result was that that many of the outdoor sessions got increasingly short to accommodate the time for a high quality review.

The complete reverse of this is of course, frontloading.

Imagine yourself on a drizzly day on the shores of Kielder Water surrounded by Europe's largest manmade forest, somewhere near the Scottish border, Northumberland, in Britain's divided kingdom standing in a small clearing on the edge of a placid lake dressed in a brightly coloured waterproof suit, with a BMX-style helmet on your head and a ludicrously bulbous buoyancy aid that looks like it's been impregnated with helium. Strewn around on mossy ground are logs, ropes, giant blue plastic barrels, different coloured canoe paddles. As you stand, fifteen ghost-faced teenage townies dressed in similar attire hover in front of you with gormless expressions that suggest they've landed on Mars or had a terminal lobotomy just because their mobile phones have been stored in a drybag. Guppy fish, await your beck and call, hopelessly in need of direction. From a birds-eye view, you might mistake this scene for a group of lost Tellytubbies the morning after an Acid House rave. The whole situation is crying out for leadership, so I break the ice with a clap and a rub of the hands, 'Raft-building, anyone?' Silence. 'Who is up for it?' Long silence. 'Yes?' 'No?' Yes!' Longer silence.

I experienced this apathy from groups most days in the 90s. Raft-building, yes, but the goal was to work as a team. To get safely across a lake without falling in. Afterwards, we'd use Kolb principles with particular accentuation on the review in what we might call the Greenaway phase. Questions in my mind were always, how could I set up their minds for the task inductively, how could I get them in the frame using some 'show' not 'tell' manner that allowed them to begin with the end in mind?

For this, I began with the 'your brain is a computer' metaphor, explaining that the human brain is subject to programming, reprogramming, and can be programmed in advance. Not that I'm a big fan of computers, but I knew how young people would relate to it quickly. Next, I'd run a physical warm-up to get their bodies and minds ready followed by a pre-framing conversation to establish expectations, set goals, and pre-empt skills. As a facilitator, my job was to ensure as little interference from me as possible on the raft building task itself and for that to be a success each student needed a clear mind-video in their heads to assume the skills for their specific role.

To do this, I'd get the group to stand like robots in a factory line and imagine they had this slot at the front of their foreheads into which they could insert a visual programme. In the early days, I got them to imagine it as a VCR video slot. In later years, this became a DVD slot. I'd get each person to fast-forward their video to the end success scene, pause it, and take a snapshot. Following that, we'd play the whole scene in reverse pausing it at crucial moments, all the way back to the start. Then we'd run it again in what felt like real time forwards to the end and pause at the moment of success. We ran the key sections forwards until all the chunks were in place and familiar, then we ran it fast-forward from the start to the end a few times asking formative questions like, 'What happens in the middle?', 'Who is doing what at the start?', and 'What's John's role near the end?' I materialised the video picture colourfully and clearly in each person's mind using brightness, contrast, and volume buttons like you would on a TV and all this pre-session effort had a positive impact on the success of the task.

Previously, before applying it, the apathy that participants initially displayed soon turned to wild enthusiasm, and certain leaders in the group who shouted loudest would take control of the situation whilst others sat on the side lines. There was a lack of confidence in the whole process, doubt, frustration, and noise, a real sense of hastiness, and invariably the raft would take off only to collapse meter from the shore. Undoubtedly, this was epic fun for the young people as it was met with raucous laughter, splashing, screaming and chaos, but preceding using frontloading as a game, group participants previously had none of this cool, calm, collectedness that, quite literally, got them to the other side.

Frontloading is a great tool to whip up mental expectation and enthusiasm and it is not restricted to kids in the outdoors. It works brilliantly if you have a family, a business, people you need to market to or individuals who need to improve skills. Frontloading can be used to set boundaries and expectations and to frame how a person will succeed in a challenge.

When You Come and See Me

Every time I think of this topic, I think of a friend of mine, who shall remain nameless, who runs a busy hypnosis school here in the U.K. This dude still offers lots of one-on-one sessions for clients, and it was on one of his hypnosis courses a few years back that I remember him talking about how he frames expectation for success with his clients. After the client has booked, he has a telephone conversation to build up their commitment. He has this phrase which he relays to them, 'When you come and see me,' as if the session is going to be really something special. He applies this also, as if he is something special, to build up expectation, and the spin-off is that the client looks forward to that day as the day when they finally make positive changes. I remember watching my friend deliver that course and giving us a demonstration on this whilst holding an imaginary smartphone, 'When you come and see me,' he said, 'you'll be totally committed.' 'When you come and see me, you won't have experienced anything like it.' At this stage, his chest started to inflate, 'When you come and see me,' now he became like a beach ball being pumped up, 'you'll get rid of your barriers in that one session.' Humorously, I relate to this as the 'When you come and see me' frame. Although I rarely use it, it always comes to mind whenever I think of ramping up the expectation.

In my personal coaching and therapy work, I have a short maxim that I use in order to get clients to pay up front and commit. 'Financial investment is emotional investment,' and 'emotional investment is financial,' meaning those who don't pay won't find a way because financial commitment is psychological commitment and, ironically, if a person hasn't invested emotionally, the financial cost of keeping their problem could end up costing them a whole lot more.

Once a client has booked, I'll consider the pre-suggestion aspect and say something like:

> 'IT's (a deliberately non-specified IT allows the client's imagination to fill in the gaps) gonna be great. LOOK FORWARD (begin with the end in mind) to YOUR (empowerment and ownership) life-changing (a presupposition of a change) session with me on [specific date and time], knowing that as each day, hour, minute, and second passes, you are already MAKING CHANGES (direct suggestion) to be FREE from [X]. And you'll know this has happened the moment you are sitting (present tense) comfortably in my big red chair (pre-hypnotic suggestion).'

Many times, it is more economical to use imagination over knowledge when setting an intention. Most of us are aware of the quote spuriously attributed to Einstein, 'Imagination is more important than knowledge,' not just because imagination encircles the world but because it bypasses interference from our conscious mind's critical faculty.

Desired future outcomes need to be congruent, highly attractive and have meaty intentions attached to them. They also need to be exciting, loaded with compelling emotion, and positive sensory stimuli.

Priming

The concept of priming is based on a psychological principle of how environmental suggestions can significantly influence our decision-making and behaviour. The suggestions can be subtle or obvious, but for the most part they are subliminal. The whole topic is very much trending in psychological circles at the moment and is being championed by people like Malcolm Gladwell, Mary Morrissey, and Robert Cialdini, who wrote the aptly named book Presuasion: A Revolutionary Way to Influence and Persuade.

The positive effects of priming can be found in studies such as the introduction of classical music on underground train systems in countries like Canada, Spain. In my own region of Tyne and Wear, the idea was first tested in the UK in the late 90s on the Metro system, also in the Elm Park district of London, where they found that within 18 months robberies were down by 33 percent, assaults on staff were down by 25 percent, and vandalism was cut by 37 percent. The sheer power of music should not be underrated. I highlighted music's influence on our actions and responses in the

Introduction when I wrote about the power of music as a suggestion when watching TV or a film.

For this book, I'd like you to view priming as subliminal sensory anchors.

I use priming all the time. When I'm running a training seminar, I want my participants calm, comfortable, relaxed, and alert. At the front of my mind is mood. What kind of mood do I want to evoke? As soon as participants step into the room, assistants greet them with warm handshakes and smiles. The first thing they smell is the coffee percolator. Snacks and fruits are nearby. The room is the perfect temperature, windows are open to allow fresh air to circulate, but it is warm and cosy.

On the wall, pictures of landscapes are festooned with quotes that reflect the intentions for the day. Wherever possible, there are flowers, chairs in open semi-circles, and an essential oil diffuser subtly blowing out fragrant wisps of peppermint or lavender. I have a small bell on the lectern so I don't have to shout to get people's attention. On the screen at the front is my name and the title of the workshop in bold along with some positive suggestion statement like LIFE CHANGING written on a flipchart.

In addition to continually honing my personal development, I remain an avid hypnotist and active hypnotherapist. Two years back, I did a home visit for a disabled woman who wanted to quit smoking. When I arrived, she apologised for the mess and informed me that the house was being decorated, that the room we were in was where she spent most of her time, and that it would be painted a warm sunny yellow colour in the morning. There were no seats in her home for me to sit on and she sat on the sofa, so I delivered a hypnosis session for her from the comfort of her wheelchair. The woman smoked over forty cigarettes a day. It was a great session, and she was a great hypnotic subject. At the end of the session I posed a post-hypnotic suggestion to seal the deal, '...and you will know that you're a healthy non-smoker now in a moment when you open your eyes...and...from this moment on now, whenever you see the colours warm, sunny, yellow.' When the woman came out of hypnosis she was crying tears of the happy kind. I pulled a little wheelie in the wheelchair, and we both rejoiced with a hug.

With that woman I had little chance to prime her environment, but framed the session on the phone, keeping in mind the late hypnotist Charles Tebbett's acronym of B.I.C.E (Belief, Imagination, Conviction and Expectation) to prepare people for hypnosis. I framed it as a bit like, 'when you come and see me,' but more of a 'when I come and see you,' as this was a home visit. I included all four elements of B.I.C.E to establish preparedness and get her in the frame for hypnosis but conclusively I it was the priming from the warm, sunny, yellow that put the cherry on the cake and nailed it for her.

When a session has been primed well, the suggestions from my hypnotic work can typically last a lifetime, years or months, but I always look to supplant environmental post-hypnotic suggestions to compliment a session. Environmental suggestions, whether it's a chair, a person, a colour, or a house pet, are incredibly powerful because they are in the immediate vicinity of the person all the time where the anchors live and are constantly being triggered.

Anchors are the stimulus responses from what we see, hear, smell, taste. They can be highly influential on our decision making. A good example is selling a house. This is a context where we'd love to influence the decision of our prospective buyers. Inside the house, we could do numerous things to prime the viewers' decisions. One thing that creates ancient, unconscious response in the wellsprings of our psyche is the smell of baked bread. Bake some bread and open the doors of suggestion.

Come on, who does not feel instantly homey the moment they smell baked bread?

Priming includes everything from the colour of your clothing, to how you look and use your voice, to the type of car you drive, to the words you use or your accent. Take voice tonality for instance, saying the exact same word or sentence in a different tonality presents us with a totally new meaning.

Priming is currently a buzzword for the subtle suggestions in our environment. I see it as an intentional, sensory-based pre-frame to get a specific result. Nonetheless, it is useful to keep in mind when we want to subliminally influence a decision, but everything in life is a suggestion.

Imaginary Lemons

You've probably heard clichés like, 'What the mind can conceive the body will achieve,' and 'The brain makes no distinction between what is real and what is imagined.' Imagine a white cup in front of you and it is there. There is the negation exercise, 'Try not to think of a pink elephant.' There is also the lemon exercise where you imagine a lemon close to your face, see its dimpled skin, notice its hue, feel its texture then imagine cutting a slice. You see a fountain of explosion, the spray from its zesty juice, you catch a whiff, bite it, and your brain engages all the physiological responses as if the lemon is actually there; as if you've bitten into it right there and then. But the lemon doesn't exist!

As the late Charles Tebbetts stated in his Rules of the Subconscious Mind, 'What is expected tends to be realised.' People who suffer from anxiety expect terror and chaos. That's what they get. Champion boxer Muhammad Ali used to perform a ritual where he'd visualise every fine detail of leaving his hotel room, from showering to getting into a taxi, walking up to the ring, and knocking out a certain opponent in a particular round. That's what he got. Elite performers don't see themselves in the starting blocks. They see themselves streaking over the finish line because they make strong associations to success.

As Napoleon Hill wrote in *Think and Grow Rich*:

To presuppose success, we must 'begin with the end in mind.'

MONITOR GROWTH

In almost all areas of life, from our work to our education to tax paying, we are held accountable. Why is this not so for your own personal growth? Why is this the lowest of our priorities? Too many folks experience a time-reality distortion when working towards their dreams. They forget where they're supposed to be going or don't realise how much they've accomplished.

Well, let's flip that on its head and put in place a small tool that helps monitor satisfaction and growth.

I'd like you to identify with your own personal satisfaction web to prove to yourself how much you are growing. Your personal satisfaction may look something like the top image on the next page.

Choose up to four key areas you want to feel satisfied in. This can be four separate areas of growth if you like, and you will score them. In this example, I have chosen money, confidence, time, and clarity.

MONITOR GROWTH

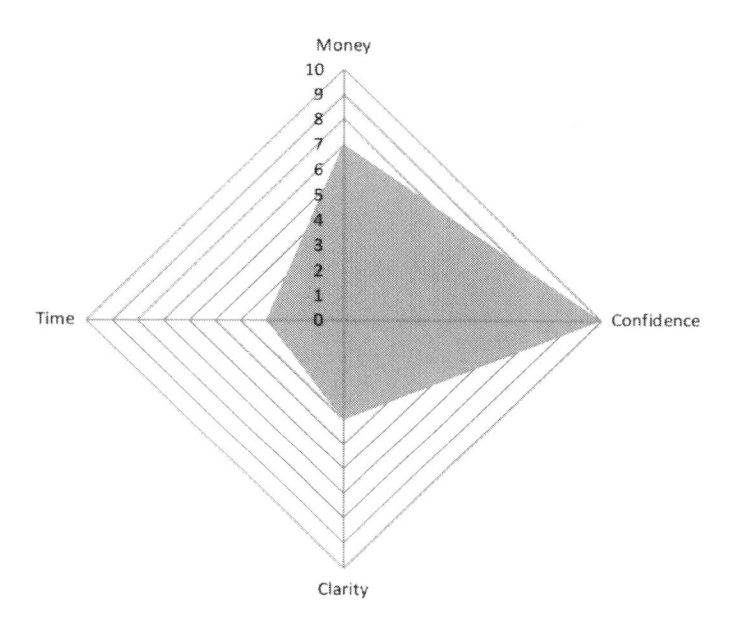

Your goal is to fill the whole web in blue, like so.

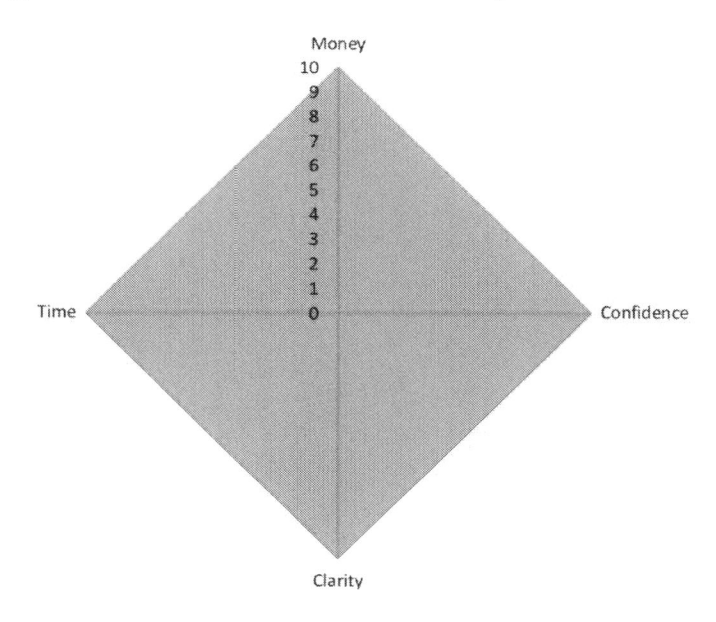

41

The ultimate goal is to get your web looking like this. Ideally, choose one key theme of your life and identify four separate areas or aspects within it. Regularly touch base with your progress (from 0 [no satisfaction] to 10 [100% satisfaction]). Make it appropriate to you, revisit every two-to-four weeks.

> Download your personal Satisfaction Web from the Maverick Mindset Skills Resources page here:
>
> http://bit.ly/MaverickMindsetSkillsFreeResources

SQUARE MINDSET VS. THE MAVERICK MINDSET

Square Mindset

Being a square is an expression people use for those who don't perform outside of the box. Squares don't do anything different. Are you a square? Here is what the fight, flee, or flop responses looks like within the Square Mindset:

FIGHT (within the context of the Square Mindset): this is the classic sense of fight, what squares do when they respond aggressively and unconsciously because of frustrated needs and desires.

FLEE (within the context of the Square Mindset): Once again, the unconscious response of a square is aversion, running away instead of facing the problem head on. Don't be square.

FLOP (within the context of the Square Mindset): This can be an unconscious or well-thought-out process in which a person experiences a 'rabbit in the headlights' reaction due to fear, anxiety, or neuro-muscular lock.

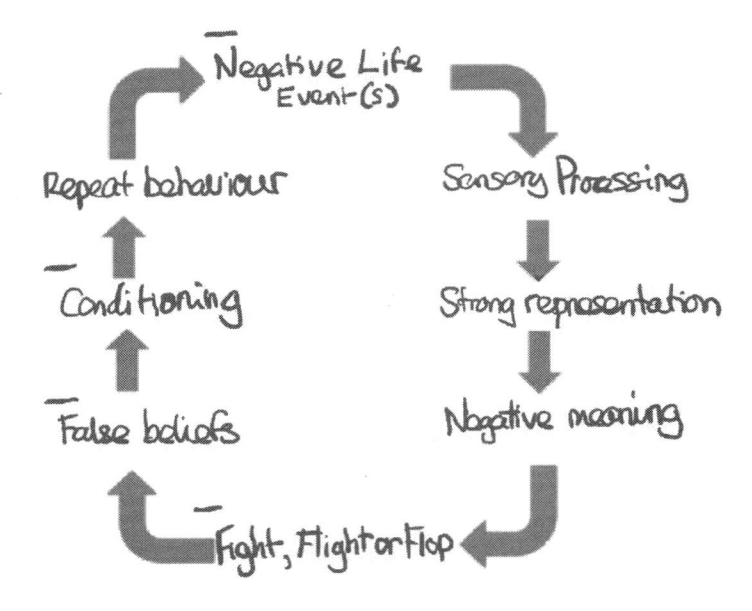

```
         → Negative Life
              Event(s)
  Repeat behaviour         Sensory Processing
         ↑                        ↓
     Conditioning          Strong representation
         ↑                        ↓
     False beliefs          Negative meaning
              ↖ Fight, Flight or Flop ↙
```

When a life event occurs, millions of bits of sensory data pass through our various lobes and filter through the channels of our five senses. This information is processed by the body's neurology, where it is converted into negative or positive meaning. This stage is a crucial phase—a choice point that predetermines our actions.

If we allow an experience to be interpreted as negative, then that's what we get. Alternatively, if we hold the initial thought at arms-length and allow it into the system only once we've interpreted it as learning, that's what we'll get instead.

Human filtering systems are like bellybuttons, biologically similar, all significantly different. Luckily, with a little awareness and predisposed thought, we can filter life's wheat from the chaff. Thought deflection using awareness can create a choice point over what comes in and stays out. Filtering preferences are subjective. How you use yours is up to you. Awareness is key. A lack awareness leaves you open to hazardous suggestions.

For example, If a crisis occurs the response might be a strong sensory representation in our minds which we feel in our bodies and, suddenly, we have blood-red terror running through our veins or strong sinking sensations that feel like a grey cloud washing over us. Visual-kinaesthetic emotional states such as these, unchecked, soon become anticipatory responses that strengthen over time into what we might refer to metaphorically as black moods or seeing red and long-term sympathetic responses such as physical constriction can soon become prolonged body pain and visible symptoms of irrational behaviour or physical change.

There is really only one choice point at the fight, flee, or flop stage. Be a terrified bunny in the headlights or create your own effective defence system to keep destructive thoughts at bay. This is not a meek process by any means. Metaphorically again, your mindset approach needs to be the equivalent of an Israeli Iron Dome system in which you intercept and obliterate each useless thought rocket before it has time to enter.

If we do nothing, we allow the rocket to land.

The negative damage is retained, it is strengthened through habitual anchoring and conditioning as recall, repeat behaviour, negative internal self-talk, and unconscious habits such as replaying the memory and formulating future disasters through the form of deceptive mind-videos.

Unaddressed, the Square Mindset brings the illusion of negative futures out on the event horizon and it's a process compounded by a cyclic nature of rinse and repeat, and because the person is experiencing life not with a sense of presence but through the lens of past conditioning, in effect, they living the past as if it's the present.

Unaltered over many years, anchoring to a no-win emotional state like this soon becomes a long period event that stays with us until our dying days.

Sadly, in many cases, people continue with their current mindset, accepting society's quick pills and fixes, going it alone, and doing the same thing the same way whilst haplessly wanting change.

As mavericks, we have choice. We have the focus and skills to control our own mind. As Mavericks, we should be doing something different to get a different result.

Maverick Mindset

Having a Maverick Mindset equips you with an easy exit

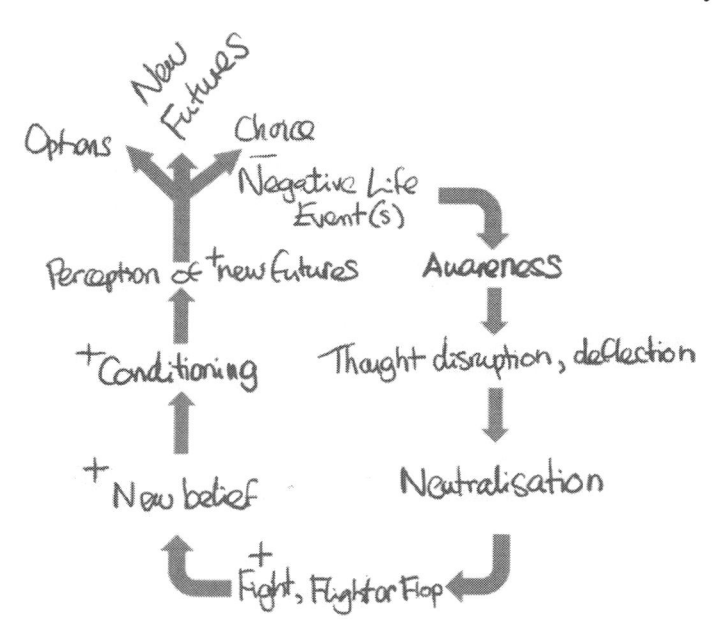

Diagram:
- Negative Life Event(s) → Awareness → Thought disruption, deflection → Neutralisation → Fight, Flight or Flop → +New belief → +Conditioning → Perception of new futures → Options / New futures / Choice

in situations of adversity. Look on it as an egress, a bypass, an outlet, an overflow, or effluence pipe for all the shit to escape.

In contrast to staying square, when a potentially negative life event occurs, we can diffuse it through cultivating light observational awareness to help us identify, divert, or dissolve potentially harmful thoughts and emotions. At this stage, the sensory representation can be neutralised from an impartial viewpoint before being given alternative meaning. Conscious processing then transforms the relationship with the fight, flee, or flop stages and uses them, now, as springboards for growth.

FIGHT (within the context of a Maverick Mindset): All emotions are valuable as long as we are in control. The Maverick fight context means you challenge convention. Anger is quickly reframed into energetic motivation. You are a catalyst of change. You never lie down. You never accept environmental impositions that do not fit your world. Instead, you use these things as fuel to change your inner and outer environments for good and stand up to injustice when others fall silent.

FLEE (within the context of a Maverick Mindset): A Maverick mind has awareness and knows that the option of moving from a dangerous or damaging environment to a place of new resource is always available. In the Maverick Mindset, with the flee option you are not refusing to face the problem; you are reframing, converting, or transforming it into something you can use in a positive and constructive way.

FLOP (within the context of a Maverick Mindset): Sometimes it is not a good idea to fight or flee. Sometimes all you need to do is sit it out, be patient, weather the storm. All things will pass...

SWITCH YOUR EMOTIONS

The ability to switch your emotions is a really critical skill. As a maverick maestro, this needs to become a part of your DNA. Ideally, you want the ability to quickly switch emotions from a potentially Square Mindset straight into the Maverick Mindset of options and choice.

A while back, I watched a program on T.V. about the SAS, the British Special Air Services. What I noticed about the SAS is that they weren't angry people that were fighting all the time. No, they were very articulate, calm, and collected individuals who could switch their emotions into a very aggressive, explosive state in an instant before turning them off and returning to a very cool, calm, and relaxed state. What defined the SAS mindset, as opposed to the average person on the street, is that the conditioning of their training had put them in control of their emotions rather than the other way around. They could shift through different emotions for task at hand. Their emotional spectrum was incredible. In hostage situations, they could switch faculties off, in other situations they could turn totally different faculties on. I found this fascinating.

Over the years, I have learnt to switch problematic emotions into the opposite context by changing my inner dialogue and the imagery in my head, also by focusing on and relaxing my muscles, changing the colour association and the movement of my feelings. Meditation certainly helps. These days it's simple, as soon as an uncomfortable thought-feeling arrives, I use the blessing of awareness to notice impartially without judgement, knowing that as long as I don't react, the cloud will pass.

Then I might ask, 'What's the opposite of that?'

All you have to do is experiment with the exercise below and familiarise yourself with making the switch fluid and elegant.

Maverick Mindset Switch

The human mind can be compared to that of a blue-arsed fly, so focused on shit that it doesn't see the jam. We've all been there. Maybe we've had multiple compliments from friends and colleagues during the course of an average day, but the moment criticism is directed our way, it catches us unaware and leaves us with a bad feeling for the rest of the day. It's a feeling that's difficult to shake off. Like flypaper, we've become attracted, stuck to it. We get so agitated that we angrily talk about it with friends but this only reinforces how stuck we feel. On some occasions it might just be that we've lost our mojo, but what do we do, we automatically drop into that mindset and stay there longer than necessary. The maverick knows that emotional states like these that we encounter in our daily lives can be flipped on their heads.

For instance, we might embark on an important task and feel ourselves getting DISTRACTED. Our mind starts wandering and we begin to lose focus. Ask, 'What's the opposite of being distracted?' The answer is FOCUS.

Sometimes we find ourselves in the DOLDRUMS. This is an old nautical term to describe when people used to find themselves stuck in the slack water of the trade winds, moving neither this way nor that. It's a great metaphor for procrastinating and being stuck. If we find ourselves in this place we ask, 'What's the opposite of being in the doldrums?' MOMENTUM.

Sometimes we are crudely aware of our own incompetence when learning a new skill. What I am talking about is CONSCIOUS INCOMPETENCE. If you experience this and think, 'I'm rubbish at this.' which can hinder progress, ask what's the opposite of that? UNCONSCIOUS COMPETENCE, the state of performing a skill so fluidly that we do it without thought. Some people call this being in the zone or a flow state. Driving a car, riding a bike, speaking, and walking are a few examples of when we apply this.

If you are experiencing LETHARGY, what's the opposite of that? ENERGY.

If you're OVER-ANALYSING, drop into the BEGINNER'S MIND.

If you feel yourself BLOCKED, elicit past events when you accessed creativity or assumed the state of creative not knowing. Revert to, 'Let's see what happens,' let your mind wonder...and wander. Give it a try, take the first step, and all of a sudden the doors will open and light will pour in. So, if you feel blocked, what's the opposite of that? CREATIVE.

You could feel yourself stuck in a Square Mindset believing that things are just IMPOSSIBLE. Start by asking, what would it be like if a miracle suddenly occurred and it all became POSSIBLE. Ask What-IF questions: what would it be like if the seemingly impossible did happen? If everything WAS possible what would I be doing then? What's the opposite of IMPOSSIBILITY = POSSIBILITY.

A big deal in the personal development world thanks to people like Tony Bobbins (yes - that was deliberate) is the notion of certainty. If you feel terribly UNCERTAIN, what's the opposite of that? CERTAINTY!

Whenever the seed of a disturbing thought creeps into our mind, before it even has the slightest chance to grow, we must switch our mindset quickly into positivity, possibility, certainty, and—vitally important—with zero ifs, buts, doubts or maybes. The switch should be fast, and the goal is to move from uncertain states and familiarise yourself with the opposite more certain states, quickly.

Three things happen when we choose to switch our emotions: One, we revive the positive states from our past to use as resources. Two, we block out what is not useful. Three, we own our response.

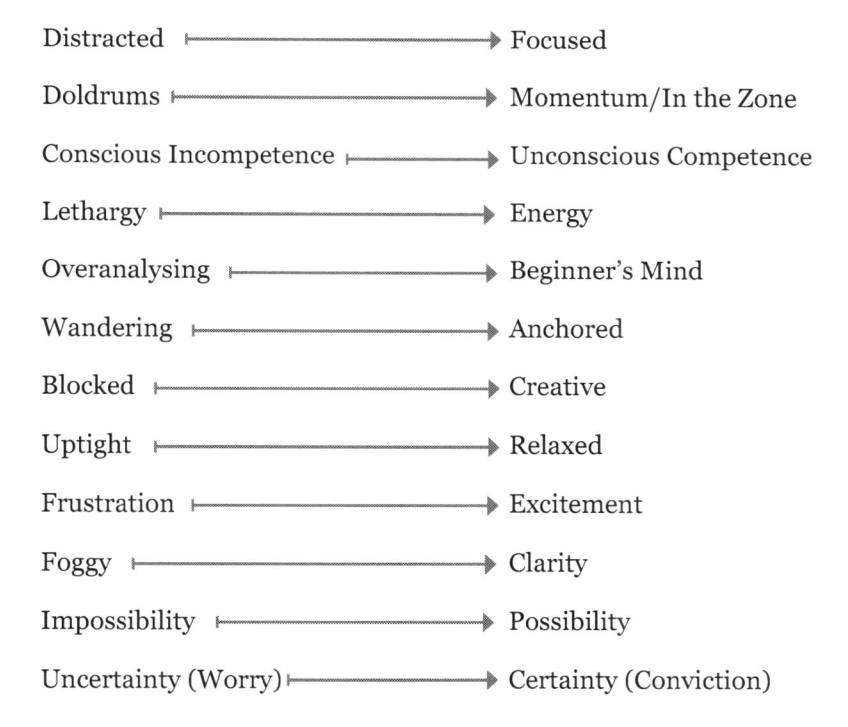

Distracted	→ Focused
Doldrums	→ Momentum/In the Zone
Conscious Incompetence	→ Unconscious Competence
Lethargy	→ Energy
Overanalysing	→ Beginner's Mind
Wandering	→ Anchored
Blocked	→ Creative
Uptight	→ Relaxed
Frustration	→ Excitement
Foggy	→ Clarity
Impossibility	→ Possibility
Uncertainty (Worry)	→ Certainty (Conviction)

I wonder, could you give yourself permission to let yourself go and allow yourself to experience only good feelings fully and completely with absolutely no resistance?

What if you started reading yourself a story about your ideal wonderful life and how things could be, and then began experiencing it in full colour, turning up the volume, introducing sensory elements like sights, sounds, smells, and feelings to make it stronger, even more memorable, and then made a commitment that you could pull this narrative out of your pocket and start believing it at any time?

Think of three of heavy emotional states that you want to change. What could these be instead? Write down your dream states on the right. Place your attention there. Run a narrative about how it COULD be IF a miracle was to occur AS IF you are experiencing that miracle now in glorious detail.

How fast can you make the switch?

Square Mindset	Maverick Mindset
These are the emotional states that are currently NOT working for you; which are currently not getting you results; the states you'd like to lose.	Remember, this is the what you would like INSTEAD context; how you would LOVE things to be IF a miracle was to occur; the opposite of your square states!
State 1 ⟶	What's the opposite of that? ⟶
State 2 ⟶	What's the opposite of that? ⟶
State 3 ⟶	What's the opposite of that? ⟶

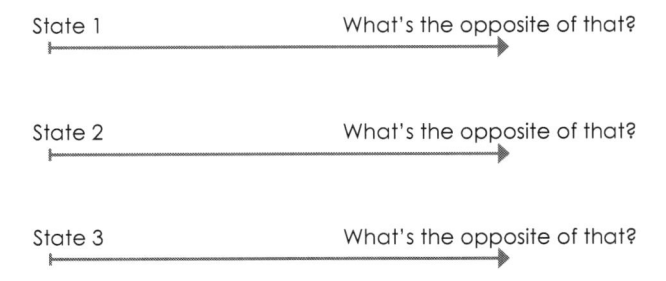

> Download your own chart for the Maverick Mindset Switch from the resources page:
>
> http://bit.ly/MaverickMindsetSkillsFreeResources

Reframing

Reframing is changing our perceptual frame, flipping our present world-view into an alternative experience. Most of the Maverick Mindset is reframing. We question how the world is presented to us to stretch current beliefs maps and do things differently to get a different result.

In essence, all Maverick Mindset Skills are reframes because we place our experience into a different frame; be it changing our attitude, our response, or our entire neurological landscape through activities, games, and exercises. There are a multitude of options. After all, our mindset is emotional state, so we can think of different contexts in which we can respond differently to the same behaviour and ask if our fear, pain, or misery would be the same if we were lying on a Caribbean beach holding the winning lottery ticket in our hand.

The frames we choose can provoke a more positive mindset through humour. By setting a humorous frame we can view our experience through a preposterously comedic lens, proposing questions like, 'I view my disappointment as if I am standing in front of a full-length mirror wearing a pink tutu and a red clown nose whilst singing Tweety Pie's 'I tawt

I taw a puddy tat.' As soon as the laughter breaks out, a reframe occurs.

What different imaginings could bring new meaning to your world? How could you relate to the same situation differently?

Reframing Language

Underestimate the power of language at your peril!

The words we use and how we use them shape our maps of the world, and language is something we could cover in more depth in a future Maverick Mindset Skills book. For now, here is a small insight into how you can quickly challenge unhelpful language and reframe it.

An example of verbal reframing could be when someone says, 'the weather's terrible today,' and you counteract it with, 'nice weather for ducks.'

In fields ranging from psychotherapy to counselling to business and sports mindset, to education, right through to our schools and the fields of self-help and personal development, we are taught that 'try' is weak word and that 'but' is bad.

For the maverick though, these are not words of weakness, failure, and negativity; a maverick doesn't listen to the masses, a maverick makes up his or her own mind and reframes terms like these for purposes of positivity.

'But' is a powerfully short linking word we can use for positive, provocative reframing by changing our phrases. Here's three scenarios in which we can use But to flip a reframe and get started:

> Everybody's greedy, BUT some people are really generous.
>
> I'm not very good at sports, BUT I'm very good at Arts and Crafts.
>
> The weather's cold here, BUT warm compared to the South Pole.

Go and find three of your own unhelpful states and see how you can flip and reframe them quickly by using the humongous power of your big fat giant BUT. Simply through changing your language like this, you begin to note the shift in internal changes of your feelings, sensory experience, and behaviour.

Reframing by Matching Language Predicates

Predicates are basically linguistic indicators of a person's experience. Words that give a clue to which one of the five senses a person is using to describe their experience.

If a person's experience is not helpful to them, by listening and watching intently, we can mirror their experience and by playing around with verbiage provoke positive reframes.

I don't want to go into it cold.	Go into it warm instead.
I'm not a very kinaesthetic person.	Wow, what an amazing feeling.
My enthusiasm goes down the drains.	Erupt into a great fount of knowledge.
Failure stinks.	What's the sweet smell of success?
I'm not a visual person.	Try not to think of a big, pink elephant.
I feel tied down.	Let's cut the ties / What frees you?
It's built on shaky foundations.	Let's get a solid, firm footing.
It doesn't chime well...	What really rings your bell?

Reframing epitomizes the maverick spirit. Most folk familiar with reframing use it loosely and only in language, but reframing is much more. In addition to linguistics, it can be used to reframe colour associations and the way feelings move in the body, internal dialogue, and the way we interpret meaning. Emotions like fear can transition into healthy excitement and stress into productivity if you keep reframing in mind.

Each one of our sensory channels is subject to reframing.

An unexpected reframe for me was once the disgusting smell of urine. By and large, the role of our unconscious minds is to keep us safe. Therefore since an early age I, hopefully like you, had always baulked at the smell of urine. It was as if my unconscious was sending me danger messages of hygiene. I probably associated the smell to vagrants and so on, but after becoming a father my association to it changed.

In certain contexts, my stimulus response changed. Having spent hundreds of hours changing my daughter's nappies when she was a baby, I learnt to desensitise my response to the smell and these days, for a fleeting moment whether in someone else's house, a community centre or shopping complex, the smell of wee-wee from babies triggers an unnervingly empathetic response. It is as if in the past I'd associated the smell to the comfort of sympathizing with my daughter's vulnerability. Of course, I know the difference between this new association and the more hazardous contexts, but I now have the benefit of appreciation as well as repulsion. After all, what excretes from our bodies is entirely natural, but the weirdness of such a response was not something I'd prepared for.

And, yes, in case you're wondering, I shower, deodorize, and change my underwear daily.

Switching Your Neuro Levels to a Maverick Mindset

As a maverick tool and the spirit of doing things different to open up new maps and stretch the boundaries of our comfort zones, I invite you to try out Robert Dilts' Neurological Levels.

Dilts was an early protégé of linguistics professor and NLP co-founder John Grinder. A pioneer and great influencer in the field of NLP, but as Mavericks we're going to address things a little differently.

I'd like you to work through his Neurological Levels in reverse with environment at the top of the hierarchy because it's contrary to how most westerners think. Environment, typically, is an afterthought. Not with mavericks, it's our highest value, because we wouldn't be here without it. A maverick also knows that before reaching a higher purpose we must first go deep.

Write your answers in the table below.

1. Think of your deepest desire, dream, or ambition, perhaps the reason why you invested time in this book.

2. Step One - for each of the six layers on the left write down what's NOT currently working in the context where your mind may feel stuck.

3. Step Two – One by one, immediately shift focus to the right-hand side for each contextual layer and write down reasonably quickly how things will look and feel like on that side for you.

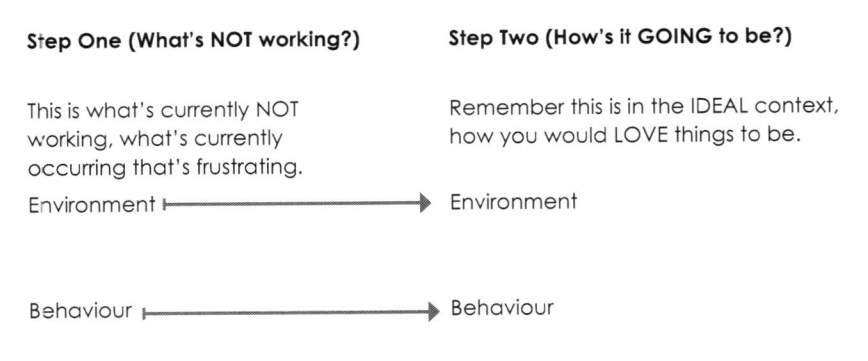

Step One (What's NOT working?)	Step Two (How's it GOING to be?)
This is what's currently NOT working, what's currently occurring that's frustrating.	Remember this is in the IDEAL context, how you would LOVE things to be.
Environment ⟶	Environment
Behaviour ⟶	Behaviour

Skills, Capabilities ⟶ Skills, Capabilities

Beliefs, Values ⟶ Beliefs, Values

Identity ⟶ Identity

Deeper Purpose, Spirit ⟶ Deeper Purpose, Spirit

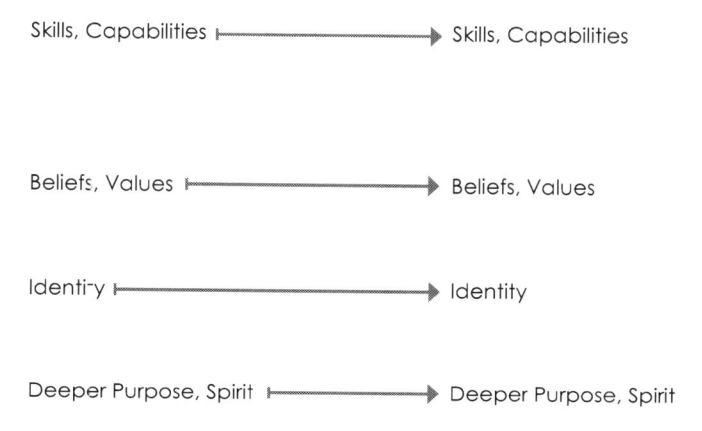

Download Switching Your Neuro Levels now from the Maverick Mindset Skills resources page here:

http://bit.ly/MaverickMindsetSkillsFreeResources

INFORMATION SORTING

When dealing with the mindset, it's never one straight route. Thanks to people like Robert Dilts and Tony Robbins, everybody nowadays seems to be referring to their ongoing growth as 'limiting' beliefs. Personally, I don't buy into that. Calling something limiting only makes it feel more limiting. Mindset change is not only about belief. Mindset change can be achieved when we overcome much more common themes like procrastination, laziness or, more often than not, a shortage in skills. In many cases, people who seek mindset coaching will arrive in their droves at your door under-confident, dissatisfied, frustrated, confused, over and under-whelmed, desperately in need of one thing: FOCUS.

Focus is the antidote, our first port of call, and recent research by Harvard University has suggested that having focus lifts our mood. Without focus, success is quickly sabotaged. Writers by nature are mavericks because they have to hold laser-focus for hours on end. Many people dream of writing a book. Most don't. Many start full of initial enthusiasm but soon find they can't hold focus. To find focus we need to S-L-O-W down, cut off mental chatter, quickly disrupt and silence it. We may have to physically apply Maverick Mindset Skills to help get in the zone or align to our highest intention. Then we list all distractions not related to our intention and remove them one by one. After that, we work on maintaining focus in that one chosen area. To sustain it, we revisit the mindset quality of Persistence: positive, patient persistence.

Logical Levels

Modern life with all its technological advancements has become extremely distracting. This makes it increasingly difficult to prioritise information and hold focus. In an ideal world, we need to be able locate, prioritise, and sort information easily to remove the confusion and chaos. We need a mind system that does it for us, a metaphoric framework if you like, to keep at the back of our minds.

In life, the ability to zoom in our conscious awareness in and zoom it out is a great gift. To think big and look small where relevant is a special skill. We need the wisdom to know when to drill down into the detail and when to move back and see the big picture. Take yourself to the start of your day when you're on a deadline to get out of the door. If you're anything like me, you might suffer from morning brain fog and struggle to direct your thoughts in a clear direction.

So, you faff, procrastinate, and get more distracted as your mind slips into the detail of a myriad of potential tasks. Do I have this receptacle for my lunch? Shall I take these? You pick up your Apple airpods. Should I make my lunch or grab a sandwich? What clothes should I wear, this or that? You're still considering small items, objects, and decisions and before you know it, you're late. This is small chunk thinking. Big picture thinking is simply, 'Get sorted—get the fuck out!' The same applies to a goal, a dream, or a business idea. Don't get lost in detail. Doing and not knowing is better than wanting to know everything and not taking action. Being a spontaneous, free and easy kind of guy who is anti-pyramid-selling and anti-greedy multi-national corporations, I am at pains to admit that we are all subject to hierarchical structures. Hidden hierarchies exist in our work and throughout society, in human models of actualisation such as Maslow's Hierarchy of Needs and Dilts' Neurological Levels, right through to lobster communities at the bottom of the ocean.

In this section we will explore an information sorting system called logical levels. Logical levels evolved from the work of an amazingly bright mathematician and philosopher, Bertrand Russell, and provide us with a clever information means of locating and itemising information in the throes of life's great matrix. Use them as modern-day principles to map ambiguity and choice.

Originally designed as mathematical principles, they can be used to understand how almost everything sits within a hierarchy of membership rules. Lauded anthropologist and social scientist Gregory Bateson, an advocate of logical levels famously espoused:

'The major problems in the world are the result of the difference between how nature works and how people think.'

You will also find logical levels in his and other books like Grinder and Bostic's Whispering in the Wind and the classic road book Zen and the Art of Motorcycle Maintenance. We work with nature, not against it.

In conjunction, if you're a manager, parent, or coach, in fact anyone who communicates with people, these principles can help, especially if a person states rather ambiguously, 'I've got a problem,' knowing about the logical levels will help you drill down to find where exactly problem lives. Does it live within the person's past, present, or future? Is it a limiting belief or an underdeveloped skill?

'What type of problem?'

'Family.'

'Okay, family.'

Then we ask, 'Is it a mother, father, spouse?' or another type of problem. The purpose of logical levels is to move from ambiguity into a set of specifics. Logical levels remain

Get Your Mind Set

in the background of our daily systems. You'll see them in education systems even technological filtering systems like Facebook ads. By understanding their existence you'll acquire more precision of mind. With logical levels we look for accuracy in the map. If you're a business person, having this awareness can help you niche and drill down for ideas. So, they are brilliant principles for communication, brilliant for business, and brilliant for organizing your mind.

An Exercise in Logical Levels

Let's assume I have a gender-neutral bag in my hand containing lots of different objects that could belong to a man or a woman. When we look at the bag we say, 'Well, it's a bag, isn't it?' But it's a diverse bag that carries lots of things in it, and if we open it up, we'll find a variety of items.

What are these things?

When we look at them, it's just stuff. Stuff we can't do much with. If we want to make decisions quickly, we'll have to organize this stuff into categories.

Let's inspect.

We've got books there, right? Paper, yeah, and a pencil case. We can call this Stationary and put it to one side. We have headphones, a phone-charger, a smartphone, and a smartphone holder.

We'll call this Technology and put it over there.

Information Sorting

I've found hand cleaner, essential oils, hand cream, Bonjela, and Tiger balm. We've got spectacles, here, to help us see and...pills...so we'll call this section Health.

Over there, I think we've got Beauty Products: eye shadow, nail varnish, foundation, lip gloss, and an intrusive memory stick to go into the Technology section.

So we've got four distinct categories: Stationary, Technology, Health, and Beauty Products. Now that's really organized things for us. We have clarity of thought and know where to place attention when we're focusing on such a big generalization as the 'items of a bag.'

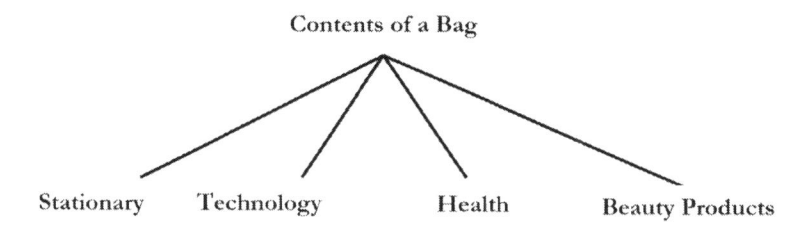

```
              Contents of a Bag
             /     |    |    \
            /      |    |     \
       Stationary Technology Health Beauty Products
```

Now we've explored the contents of a bag and separated them into different sets, let's focus more closely on just one logical type: Technology. Let's drill even deeper to get more pinpoint precision. By zoning in with laser-type accuracy beyond the set membership rule of Technology, we focus our attention on one subordinate type, Data Storage.

Let's look at how the set membership rule applies to an ambiguity such as Data Storage. Chunk down and we find three categories: Internal Data Storage, External Data Storage and, say, 'other' Data Storage.

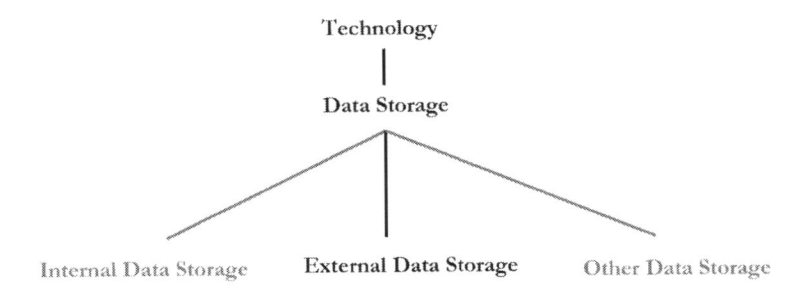

```
                    Technology
                        |
                   Data Storage
                   /    |    \
                  /     |     \
    Internal Data Storage   External Data Storage   Other Data Storage
```

If we choose only one category, External Storage, we'll find Memory Sticks, External Hard Drives, and Cloud Systems, which are all separate logical types.

```
              External Data Storage
               /       |       \
              /        |        \
       Memory Sticks  Hard Drives  Cloud Systems
```

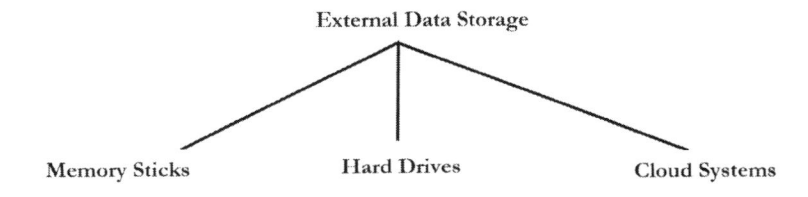

Bateson also critiqued NLP as shoddy epistemology and coined a saying, 'You are comparing apples to oranges,' a phrase which became synonymous in NLP, personal development, and business circles as a means to point out when two items are polar opposites. This metaphorical quip refers to how set memberships of categorisation are created and within them are distinctly separate logical types. Apples and Oranges both come under the same set membership rule of Fruit but remain contrastively different in type. Few folk would display tomatoes in fruit bowls in their lounge even though they are fruit. That's because they are different. This is what Bateson described as the 'difference that makes a difference.'

Logical Types

People are a fantastically diverse example of logical types. In my personal life I prefer hanging out with fruit as it's much less high-maintenance, nonetheless, people types make a fascinating study. Let's have a look at how we can organise people information into types on good old LinkedIn. Promoted as the world's biggest social networking platform for professionals with over 660,000 million users in over 200 countries, LinkedIn is a fine environment to see the logical levels in action.

For example, we can search certain types of people in certain roles, in certain parts of the world with certain job titles, it's perfect. First, we begin by visiting 'my network,' top of the page. Click that. Left, if we click on 'connections,' I find I have 17,321 connections, so I go to the search bar on the right and click 'search with filters.' A big search bar pops up top left with a number of options. We are going to look for 'people,' so I click on that.

People

'People' is too vague because we haven't got any locations, connections, companies, or anything like that yet. We still want to get tighter, so I avoid 'second connections,' because that would include the connections of my current connections and be quite broad. So I go ahead and click 'first connections,' the people with whom I'm currently connected. Already, we're down to a tidy 16,713 results.

First Connections

I begin to chunk down a little by inputting the job title of 'Coach' and see 7,595 connection results.

Coach

We can chunk down some more to the logical type of Executive Coach; that's still quite vague but better because I've now got 4, 094 results.

Executive Coach

So let's trim this down a bit. Let's look at 'location,' and put in Spain. We press apply, and now we're down to 291 results.

Spain

To trim further, I remove 'Spain' and put 'Madrid area Spain' as a specific location, and now I'm down to only 117 Executive Coaches. Perfect! Now we can focus our attention on a manageable group of people with whom I can communicate and form personal pro-social relationships.

Madrid

As we move down the tree, this process of reduction is called constriction as the numbers and items become fewer. To summarise, we've pointed our attention to Executive coaches living in Madrid, Spain, to whom I'm already

Information Sorting

connected to. Keeping the logical levels in mind can help us get razor sharp, laser-focused, and crystal clear. Use them as a roadmap to match cold scientific realities with warm romantic dreams. Move beyond living on a hope and a whim, organise your mental maps, and get yourself practical with measured results.

As you can see, you'll need to dance between big-picture and small-picture perspectives to maximise mindset success. Relying on the fibs of books like The Secret and willpower alone can be exhausting and demoralising, and this is exactly how I used to behave. Many years ago, during the late 1970s, I used to rush home after school to eagerly turn on the TV and watch a programme called Why Don't You? When the music came on there was this cartoon image of a bored kid slumped in a chair and the programme started with a song, 'Why don't you, Why don't you...go out and do something less boring instead.' As the lyrics came to a close 'sitting at home watching TV, turn it off it's no good to me,' suddenly the boy put his foot right through the telly. I was that boy. I still am to some degree because I've never been lazy, I've always been motivated, but without a clear plan. Late in the 80s, I used punk rock as my emotional state motivator. I used to play songs from my LP collection like Fugazi's Waiting Room and Canadian hardcore band SNFU's, Get Off Your Ass, crank up the volume, and go out to unleash my mission on the world. SNFU stood for Situation Normal Fouled Up. In that vein, I got out of the waiting room but my situation remained fouled up because I had no idea what my mission was or how to implement it. This frustrated me like hell. I kept getting off my arse with real intent but kept hitting a wall. Directionless, I'd hover spasmodically in parks and public spaces on a diet of music and hope. That's how it's been most of my life.

Notwithstanding my younger muggy thinking, this intentional energy lies at the heart of the Maverick Mindset, passion and desire, because there comes a time when we've had enough of the crap, when we cross the threshold, and the time calls for change. By taking ourselves to this threshold we can deliberately arouse the overwhelming emotions that explode us into action and shove us over the line. Deliberately, we arrive can toss on the fabled 'last straw' so that we reach a point of emotional release that has us yelling from the rooftops—'THAT'S ENOUGH!'

My ambiguous view of the world did not yield major results for me. I needed a map. A system. A plan. You see, the romantic views the world through a rose-tinted fog. The scientist sees it through the sterile view of his microscope. The maverick sees through both of these lenses and more. While the maverick likes pinpoint precision and fact he or she also holds a soft romanticism to feel beyond the restriction of microscopes.

So rather than faff and procrastinate, get off your arse, go out and do something less boring instead, but this time with

Information Sorting

a map, compass a map, and head torch. Begin thinking of ways now in which you can apply this chunking system not as a rule but in principle to your life and work. Like anything, it's a map, and before it was created it didn't exist.

Don't take the idea of putting people into types too seriously either. Categories and types come with a caveat: do not to take literally. Categorizing and typing is an exercise in awareness and bringing organisation to abstract thought. I wouldn't want you going around saying 'he's this type,' and 'she's this type,' as personality profiling conflicts with the maverick mind.

A maverick understands the nature of life—uncertain—the maverick revels in uncertainty, embraces it as an opportunity for creativity. Nor are mavericks on red alert for seeking out labels for themselves or others as fixed types for such an approach would prevent us from seeing that commonalities are greater than difference.

In the words of John Lydon in his book with a fabulous reframe in the title, *Anger Is An Energy*, when he talks about people attempting to define punk, 'We've got to learn to stop thinking in terms of categories as species. This is that and that's that. No, there's cross-pollination all the time.'[1] Rules are there to be noticed, not to be believed. So that, my friends, was logical levels. I hope this helped. If it did, great. If it didn't, no problem. I don't give a shit.

---

[1] Lydon, John & Perry, Andrew. 'The Boy Don't Surrender', *Anger Is An Energy*. Simon & Schuster, (London, UK, 2014). p. 166-167

UNCERTAINTY, YOUR FRIEND

In the past I have heard people jest, 'The only certainties in life are death and taxes.' What a load of old bunkum. What a pile of old pants. Some fiscal deviants avoid taxes and shift them abroad. Large corporations employ high-level accountants and lawyers to exploit legal loopholes so that they can avoid taxes.

Certainty is a mythical concept. Everything in life is uncertain. You could say that the only true certainty in life is that life will remain uncertain. Although we may experience sensations of certainty from time to time that lull us into a sense of security, things very rarely go as planned.

Change is reality. Nature is change. If we don't respect continuous change, we may begin to feel the effects of the human-nature disharmony I touched on earlier with Bateson's quote. Most of humanity's problems stem from the difference between how nature works and how people think.

The tallest and oldest trees in the forest are the most flexible. Life is easier when we learn how to flex with natural laws than when we become blinded by our beliefs and by a false sense of certainty. Rather than pining for certainty, freaking out at unforeseen change, or expecting reality to bend for us, we can better expend our energies by learning how to flex with reality.

Certainty and uncertainty are feelings. They are abstract concepts, not things. Yet, we treat them as if they are nouns. Certainty is impermanent. Uncertainty is unpredictable. In fact, death is the only absolute certainty.

Don't Fear the Reaper

So, let's focus on the merry old subject of death for a while.

Death.

Is there a more unavoidable way to push yourself towards positive imminent action? Is there a more inescapable way to motivate oneself? Is there a more impending challenge to acquire the Maverick Mindset?

Let's get this straight. I don't see death as a gory, Evil Dead II scenario where I'm being chased by my own severed hand. No, I see it as honest, and I remain curious as to how, where, and when mine will happen. I don't know where I will go when I die, but the one thing I know with absolute certainty is that death is inevitable.

Death.

From the moment you're born, the parking meter starts ticking. When you're young, you don't hear it. Days and weeks seem like years as they pass, but as you get older, the ticking gets faster and louder. There's probably not a day goes by when I do not think about my own death. But even the certainty of death contains uncertainty, as we can never ascertain exactly how, when, or where it's going to happen.

Death.

It worries, scares, fascinates, and motivates me. As I get older, it gets closer each day. Death. It challenges me to take chances on my life plans, knowing that any long-term strategies could all be in vain.

Death.

I wrestle with this conundrum each week. Do I stick to my longer-term vision, investments, and frameworks or abandon it all in a millisecond to become a spendthrift, dance naked in the streets, and live for each individual minute? It's this annoying, 'I could get run over by a bus tomorrow...' syndrome that conflicts with everyday future planning and the personal legacy I want to leave behind. But for now, I've decided to embrace this little dance with death.

Death.

Most people ignore death.

They push it away, only for it to come and haunt them on their dying day, and those who ignore death right up until they actually have to face it often find they encounter it with a feeling of, 'Why me?' or 'This shouldn't be happening,' because up until this point they've ignored death for so long.

A few years back, a Buddhist friend of mine was going through the dying process when I noticed something of interest. Right through the build-up to him crossing over, I watched him maintain a peaceful state of calm and a positive acceptance of his death. Perhaps this was the result of meditations in Buddhism that get people conditioned to death as a means of appreciating reality. Imagine being fearless and peaceful at the time of your death so that you pass away with contentment. I find this equally unusual and interesting.

Awareness of death awareness brings a quality of appreciation and honesty to our lives, and the Buddhist approach is the exact opposite of how we view death in the West. In the West, it is quite common for people to die with psychological pain, attachment to ideals, or with unresolved family feuds. Many people in the West depart life alone, in fear, or with terrible regret. Australian author Bronnie Ware wrote candidly in her book The Top Five Regrets of the Dying about the insights she had during her work in palliative care. She groups these insights under themes like: I wish I hadn't worked so much. Bizarrely, none of these regrets had anything to do with money, even though that's what society hypnotises us to strive for much of our working lives.

When people visit my website, my Facebook business page, or my LinkedIn profile, they often say, 'Oh, I see you're a life coach?' 'No,' I say, 'I'm a death coach.' I coach you how to celebrate life's ONLY certainty. When faced with the reality of death, living a life of real meaning becomes that much more urgent, so we never waste a single day. Instead, the maverick identifies the threat from potential regrets and uses them as springboards to take positive imminent action. The intention is that as we come to the end of our days, instead of feeling regret, we look back and say, 'Boy, what a journey. What a ride.'

Mourning Celebrations

When a loved one dies in the West, tradition has it that the family of the deceased wears black, grows sombre, and slumps into a pit of blackened sorrow during the funeral and for long after the loved one has passed. The Irish approach to death is more fun. Check out the late Dave Allen's comedy sketch on YouTube on what death means to the Irish. In some parts of Ireland, they still engage in the age-old tradition of merrymaking. What would it be like to attend your best mate Paddy's funeral, and after the initial lamenting with Paddy's lifeless body in the open coffin, you look on as someone props him up in the corner with a pipe hanging out of his mouth and bottle of whiskey shoved in his hand. Laughter, singing, poetry, and the sound of musical accompaniments fill the air whilst the mourners rejoice his life.

In Tarot, the death card represents a new beginning. That's why death is maverick and why viewing it in this light is the greatest reframe of all. This section was originally going to be called 'Death to the Maverick' because I wanted to showcase the benefits of contrarian thinking. As an aside, 'Death to the Maverick' is also what people will shout when you embrace your true spirit and dare to do what's different. This is human nature. People often meet concepts that challenge the status quo with jealousy and retribution. People freak out when things change. They lash out at anything that doesn't fit their current belief map. But rocking the boat is essential. There's nothing antagonistic about it either, particularly if you want to stand up for justice or if you believe in being authentic. A real maverick knows the beauty of a switch in perspectives, for what one culture laments, another celebrates. Therefore, you do not give a shit. You must not give a shit. Use your death as the flaming torch that ignites your positive actions. Feel death pressing on your back. Let it be your motivator. Replace the phrases 'maybe later' or 'one fine day' with 'now,' 'let's do this,' and 'today,' in full knowledge that the greatest wisdom comes from doing. Begin with the end in mind, before you're ready. Apply curious effort, and get off your arse and do something. Get your mind set today before the parking meter finally stops ticking...

Necessity is Essential

Certainty doesn't exist. Feelings of certainty, yes ? but actual certainty, no. If we long to feel certain more often, we can work with our inner emotional state to deliberately evoke feelings of certainty by identifying the apparent certainties in our life like our name, where we were born, a belief, a holiday where we felt connected, or a statement of obvious fact. If certainty is what you want, simply familiarise yourself with feelings of certainty more often and, that's right, you'll start to feel more certainty.

One thing that really brings us a sense of certainty is confidence. Confidence is the acquisition of skills, especially at the unconscious competence phase. Productivity comes from when we have found our rhythm and are in the zone, receiving neurological reward from our micro-goal achievement. But for this to happen, we first need to set the conditions of success and balance them out by creating positive frameworks, clockwork-like systems, and rituals that help us convert abstraction into positive physiological, neurological, and spiritual feedback.

Buddhists meditate. Turkish Sufis perform the Whirling Dervish. Christians pray. Muslims perform the act of fasting. All are rituals that embed a skill or belief. Think of these rituals like anchors for our feelings of certainty that help us carve maps into places where a map may not have previously existed. Most concrete outcomes in the material world are based on processes of deliberation and iteration. So, bind yourself into these with a certain degree of fear for what the consequences will be if you don't do them because if you truly, absolutely, want to achieve one special thing in your life more than anything else, then rituals aren't necessary, they're absolutely effing essential.

In NLP there is a linguistic mouthful called 'the modal operators of necessity' which identify when a person has bound themselves into an unproductive set of language patterns. Language patterns like these usually arise from some childhood belief or enforced values system. The modal operators of necessity consist of expressions like: 'I must,' 'I should,' 'I ought to,' 'I need to,' 'I've got to,' 'I have to,' and when used repeatedly over time these expressions act as linguistic binds that strengthen the stuck mindset within the individual. Probably because they had slid into this default state, it increases their discomfort and inaction. NLP practitioners are taught to challenge these spells and break the unconscious binds using a language pattern called the Meta Model. In therapeutic counselling and personal development, we are often taught to completely delete the modal operators of necessity from conversation or internal dialogue and replace them with positive alternatives such as, 'What if...I could,' 'What if...I had?' 'I have,' 'I will,' and 'I am.'

Anyhow, NLP originated in California, but the maverick approach originates elsewhere. The Maverick Mindset is bold as brass, with a grime and grit that comes straight from the pits and slagheaps of a wintry northern town where the women wear stilettos and bikinis in sub-arctic temperatures and grown men expose their tattooed beer bellies at football matches whenever their team scores a goal.

This Maverick Mindset is most probably the opposite of possibility-based Californian NLP. I'll admit, Californian NLP did have a maverick edge, that's what appealed to me in the first place all those years back, but it was largely about exploring possibility, the sunny life of hippie freedom, increasing our options and choice. For the most part this is good, but the Maverick Mindset derives more from an Eric Burdon, the lead singer of The Animals, wisdom. Eric, a man from my part of the world, understood this underdog spirit perfectly when in 1965 he wrote the song, 'We Gotta Get Out of this Place.' You could hear his environment in his voice. Like Eric, the Maverick Mindset is about shining a light 'in a dirty old part of the city where the sun refuses to shine.' It's a mental toughness built on desire, strong work ethics, and industrial ingenuity. Only through adversity do we find our best solutions to prosper against all odds, and much of the time this occurs through necessity, where there is an apparent lack of choice.

Choice.

The maverick's choice is to remove it.

Choice is mostly useful at the brainstorming phase, and feelings of certainty come from consistently holding our focus to consistently maintain our results. Focus means holding our attention in one particular area and keeping going. Once we have made our decision to commit, we remove all irrelevant distractions and tell ourselves what we must, need, or have to do. We grit our teeth and march on.

Why would an Olympian get out of bed at 4:30 a.m. and perform this same ritual every day, even when they have deep family concerns or experience loneliness, inner doubt, and physical pain in all manner of conditions from blistering heat to icy miserable rain? Do you think their inner dialogue is saying: 'I have a few different choices here and one of them is lying in bed. The other is to not do this at all or postpone it for a later date. I could always watch TV or have a duvet day.' No — they remove the choice and the options to opt out. That's what keeps them consistent, optimal, and on track. They 'have to,' and that's what they say in order to achieve beyond the ordinary. That one, single, bloody-minded vision.

Why do millionaires get up every morning at a specific time and complete tasks to a highly specific order?

If you work for an employer, the same applies to you. Why do you rush out of bed, wreak havoc in the house, and rush out the door with a half-bitten piece of toast in your mouth and your hair blowing all over the place? Why might you spend a long time at a specific time every single day to look smart at your work? Because you have to, and if you don't, you will probably end up getting the sack. If you get the sack, you may lose your house, your car, your child's education, or worse: your sanity or your ability to afford food.

Why do soldiers go to war on only three hours sleep in two days and little food?

They 'have to,' and this is exactly what their internal dialogue says in order to override doubt when they start thinking, 'I can't go on' or 'I don't think I can do this.'

When we deliberately place binds on ourselves like this, awareness is key. Sometimes we need choice, sometimes we don't, so using the modal operators of necessity like this, in reverse and with wisdom, will give you a significant advantage, increase results, and get you more feelings of certainty.

Also, on the path to achieving something specific and important, once we've aligned with our highest value and ruled out all other options, using uncomfortable binds in this way will intensify our commitment to the cause.

'Effortless' is not without effort. And guess what? If you don't 'have to,' you probably won't. If you want to just feel good about yourself whilst doing absolutely nothing, I strongly recommend studying the Law of Attraction. The Maverick Mindset is different.

The maverick guy or gal sometimes uses uncomfortable binds as springboards of positive necessity. If you are not a dreamer and are genuinely serious about achieving your passion and leaving that one proud legacy you are proud of so you, too, can rest on your deathbed at peace, the very first step is to attach strong emotion and commitment to your desire.

Only after we've achieved that dream, and reaped the reward of our dopamine fix and the deep satisfaction that comes with it, may we look back through a much softer lens to reflect on how we handled the variety of choice.

That's why you need to, you must do, you should, and you have to. Behaviours and actions are driven by our values and beliefs. If you believe that you should, must, need to, and have to, it's most likely that you probably will.

FUTURE DIARY

Before you dash off and sort all your shit, I'd like you to create something that will supplant your visions, goals and objectives into an encouragingly supportive framework for your mind.

A methodology with which you can start to plan all the things in advance that you want to experience, see, hear and feel in the future that have everything to do with your strongest positive intention.

By reverse-engineering your future, this will help materialise your long-awaited dreams. If 'the law of attraction is physical action,' then map out your dream vision in reverse to turn it into physical reality.

Maybe you're aware of the method for writing a letter from your future self. That's useful too, but a future diary is a process by which you plan the weeks, months, and years from the end of having achieved that dream in reverse.

Write this on a notepad or create it electronically.

Write how you feel in the present tense having achieved your dream. Fill each block with words, drawings, imagery, cut-outs from magazines, whatever amplifies the attachment to your goal. Set a specific timeframe whether this is days, weeks, months, or years ahead.

Apply all six levels of Dilts' neurological levels as a hierarchy for your progression if you like. Likewise, use Russell's logical levels to create big picture viewpoints and locate necessary detail, be as simple or as creative as you like.

Start writing your future (diary) today.

MAVERICK MINDSET QUIZ

Go through the Maverick Mindset Quiz below and circle or tick your answers to the questions. Once you've done that, you can check your answers at the back. No cheating!

1. How do the logical levels help you get your mind set? (one answer)

    a. By using your emotions as drivers.
    b. By shifting your focus and attention.
    c. By helping you focus and sort information.

2. Why should you use imagination when goal setting or moving towards an intention? (one or more correct answers)

    a. Beginning with the end in mind presupposes success.
    b. Future attractions need strong emotions and intentions.
    c. What is expected tends to be realised.
    d. The brain makes no distinction between what is real and what is imagined.
    e. What the mind can perceive, the body will achieve.

MAVERICK MINDSET QUIZ

3. Why is it important to not give a shit about what others think of you? (one or more correct answers)

    a. As a maverick maestro, you will need to put yourself 'out there' to make a positive difference.
    b. Fear of criticism and rejection is one of the primary barriers for not taking action.
    c. Your future success relies on positive persistent action.

4. Why is it best to shift our mind into the opposite frame, quickly keeping our attention there and specifically NOT talking about or imagining what went wrong in problem contexts? (one correct answer)

    a. Being silent is best.
    b. Whatever the mind relives or revives makes it stronger.
    c. Einstein has a theory on this that makes it true.

5. What are the key Maverick mindset qualities? (one correct answer)

    a. Planning, Preparation, Prevention, Performance.
    b. Aversion, Constriction, Denial, Comfort Zones.
    c. Intention, Positivity, Curiosity, Persistence, Don't Give a Shit.

6. What is the best way to combat repeated failure inside the square mindset? (one correct answer)

    a. Keep trying the same way but use more force.
    b. Stay flexible, learn from the experience, then try a different approach.
    c. Call a friend for support and talk for hours about how unfair the world is.

7. Which statement is the most appropriate description of the Maverick mindset? (two or more correct answers)

   a. The Maverick mindset is about growing material wealth.
   b. The Maverick mindset is about growing your skillset, mindset, and neurology.
   c. The Maverick mindset is about getting more things.
   d. The Maverick mindset is about creatively doing things differently to get a different result.
   e. The Maverick mindset is about increased academic intelligence.

8. Why does a Maverick Mindset value the prospect of death? (two or more correct answers)

   a. The prospect of death motivates us towards positive imminent action.
   b. A 'romantic' view does not always lead us to action.
   c. Fear and morbidity will lead us to action.
   d. Being mindful of death keeps us in tune with reality.
   e. Death aligns us with life's only certainty.

Answers to Quiz

1. By helping you focus and sort information.

2. Beginning with the end in mind presupposes success.

    Future attractions need strong emotions and intentions.

    What is expected tends to realised.

    The brain makes no distinction between what is real and imagined.

    What the mind can perceive the body will achieve.

3. As a Maverick maestro, you will need to put yourself 'out there' to make a positive difference.

    Fear of criticism and rejection is one of the primary barriers for not taking action.

    Your future success relies on positive persistent action.

4. Whatever the mind relives or revives makes it stronger.

5. Intention, Positivity, Curiosity, Persistence, Don't Give a Shit.

6. Stay flexible, learn from the experience, then try a different approach.

7. The Maverick mindset is about growing your skillset, mindset and neurology.

The Maverick mindset is about creatively doing things differently to get a different result.

8. The prospect of death motivates us towards positive imminent action.

    A romantic view does not always lead us to action.

    Being mindful of death keeps us in tune with reality.

    Death aligns us with life's only certainty.

Want to get clear on your big idea, the mindset, model and method? If you haven't already, check out my crash course in confidence directly:

https://bit.ly/OnlineConfidenceCrashCourse

Nicky!

"You have tremendous skill, care and compassion. Keep pushing the boundaries and never stop growing!"

All the best,

Joey — July 2020.

Printed in Poland
by Amazon Fulfillment
Poland Sp. z o.o., Wrocław